'Pint to Pint - More Pub In The South Hams

by
Robert Hesketh

ORCHARD PUBLICATIONS
2 Orchard Close, Chudleigh, Devon TQ13 0LR
Telephone: (01626) 852714

ISBN 1 898964 70 X

Printed by
Hedgerow Print, Crediton, Devon EX17 1ES

Contents

INTRODUCTION

Making a second selection of South Hams walks to follow my first *Pint to Pint* has proved very enjoyable. There is no better way to explore this beautiful area of Devon than on foot. Indeed, much of it, especially the coast, can only be explored by walking. The South Hams offers a magnificent variety of scenery, as well as many attractive villages and towns. It also has many fine inns, full of historic interest. Each of the circular walks in this book features at least one inn, chosen for its history, atmosphere, good food and (not least!) real ale.

The walks vary from a modest 5km/3 miles to a full day's 14.5km/9 miles. Some are more demanding than others, thus steep ascents/descents and the numbers of stiles en route are listed as a gauge. Please read the notes at the head of each walk before starting, particularly information on ferries and tides.

Whether you choose a long or a short walk, suitable clothing, walking boots, and drinking water are essential. So too is the Ordnance Survey's Outdoor Leisure 20 map, which covers all the routes and contains far more helpful detail, including field boundaries, than was possible on the Landranger 202. I recommend taking a walking stick, extra food, mobile phone and map case too. For added interest bring binoculars – the South Hams is rich in bird life and you may well spot dolphins, porpoises or seals along the coast and estuaries.

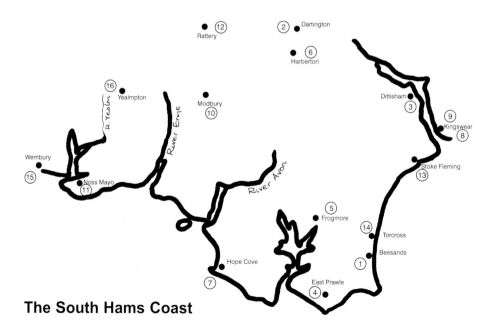

The South Hams Coast

1. BEESANDS AND HALLSANDS FROM THE CRICKET INN, BEESANDS. 9km (5½ miles) OR 11km (7 miles) WITH START POINT.

Start/parking: sign-posted parking area facing the beach at Beesands, SX820405.
Suitable for: anyone fairly fit.
Terrain: well signed coast path, footpaths and quiet lanes. Some ups and downs, but no really demanding gradients.
Stiles: 1
Start Point Lighthouse: Normally open Easter to end September. Daily during July and August (11am-5pm) and Wednesdays, Thursdays, Sundays, Bank Holidays and school half-terms for the rest of the time. Confirm on 01803 770606. www.trinityhouse.co.uk

In calm weather or in storm, Start Bay is equally impressive and this walk gives a fine panorama of a great bite of land claimed by the sea. From the lighthouse at Start Point in the south to Combe Point in the north is eleven and a half kilometres (over seven miles) as the crow flies. Parts of Start Bay are protected from the sea's fury and easterly storms by high cliffs; other sections are poorly defended.

We set off from the sea wall at Beesands and walk on to Hallsands, a fishing village built on a raised beach and largely destroyed by the sea. As the path curves south to Start the full drama of the seascape opens out. By adding an extra 2km to the route you can visit Start Point and enjoy a guided tour of the lighthouse.

Our return route follows quiet lanes and byways. Some of these are ancient and have been eroded into the earth over centuries to form *hollow ways*, with banks ten feet high or more in places. Little used today, they tend to be overgrown in summer – a walking stick may be handy.

1. Start/parking: Follow the sea front past the Cricket Inn. Bear right at the coast path sign for Hallsands. Walk uphill to a path junction. Bear left to follow the coast path, which is easy and largely level, to North Hallsands. Turn right in front of the ruined building and climb the steps to Trout's, which offers a range of refreshments.

Opposite is a viewing platform, which is as close as visitors are allowed to the remains of South Hallsands because of cliff falls. Plaques and period photographs tell the story of how *The beach went to Devonport and the cottages went to the sea,* (Kingsbridge Gazette, 1917).

1

South Hallsands was once a thriving community of 73 houses and 128 people, with its own pub, post office and grocery. However, much of it was destroyed by a storm in 1917. The underlying cause of this may well have been dredging. 650,000 tons of shingle had been removed from the protecting Skerries Bank in Start Bay to extend Devonport Dockyard some years earlier, making the low lying village especially vulnerable.

2. 2km (1¼ miles) Return to the coast path, which becomes steeper. A few stunted trees bent by the wind testify to its force, a force that has wrecked many ships over the centuries. Local wrecks include the *Lunesdale,* a 141 ton three-masted schooner destroyed in the Great Blizzard of March 1891 and the *Crown Prize*, a twenty six gun man o' war, run aground in an easterly gale in 1692. Both met their end at Beesands.

South Hallsands today - apart from the houses in the foreground most have been claimed by the sea.

When the steamer *Newholm* was sunk by a German mine in that fateful year of 1917 off Hallsands, Devon found its own 'Grace Darling'. Twenty year old Ella Trout saw the disaster when she was crabbing and rowed out immediately. Another local fisherman, William Stone, also rowed to the scene. Between them, Ella and Stone saved nine men. Ella Trout was later awarded the O.B.E. The parents of one of the men she saved gave her money in gratitude. Ella and her sisters had been made homeless by the storm earlier the same year, so they put the money towards buiding the Trout's Hotel we have just visited.

3. 3.25km (2 miles) To extend your walk to the lighthouse from the car park, simply follow the tarmac drive ahead for 1km (¾ mile) and return. 87 feet (28m) tall, Start Point lighthouse has warned ships about one of England's most exposed peninsulas since 1836. Now fully automated, it casts a beam twenty five sea miles.

Follow the tarred lane from the car park to Hollowcombe Head Cross.

4. 5km (3 miles) Turn right for South Hallsands and then first left for Lamacraft Farm. From there, continue ahead on the public byway as signed. This leads downhill to a footpath junction. Walk ahead on a tarred track to cottages. Leave the track, which bears left, and continue ahead on a wide, grassy path.

This path leads to a lane. Turn left. 250m ahead, bear right onto the byway for Higher Middlecombe. Ignore the later side turning for Hallsands. From Higher Middlecombe, walk ahead as directed by the red arrows. The byway enters a tarred track. Turn right and first right again at the waymark for Beesands.

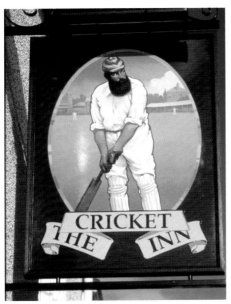

5. 7.25km (4½ miles) This path is not clearly delineated on the Ordnance map, but nonetheless forms a clear route with hedges on the left and offers a fine view of Start Point. At another waymark, it turns sharp left and descends to the coast path. Bear left and follow the coast path back to Beesands.

The village once had two pubs. Henry Crocker and his wife, Susanna, ran the King's Arms, which opened in 1826 and closed in 1910, but the first reference to the Cricket Inn was in 1867. Visitors might assume that the recent sign, depicting a sailing vessel, was connected with the inn's name, but this is not so. The present sign of a cricket player (based on W.G. Grace, famous for his batting and prodigious beard) probably has more historical validity. Indeed, a number of inns up country are named after cricket. The first was recorded in 1804 and associated names such as Umpire, Pavilion and Bat and Ball are by no means unusual.

Although one Captain Fredrick Cricket lived at Hallsands, it is extremely unlikely that the inn was named after him as he was born in Plymouth in 1855. Thus, he would have been only twelve years old and unknown locally when the Cricket Inn was first recorded! The Cricket Inn was then run by Philip Prettyjohn who later moved to Hallsands to run the London Inn - which was wrecked by the sea in 1904, an early victim of dredging. Prettyjohn's daughter, Elizabeth Ann, was born here in 1883. She was the one of the last inhabitants of South Hallsands.

The Cricket Inn is decorated with old maps, charts and an excellent assortment of local photographs, one of the best pub collections in the South Hams and a really valuable historical record. These show local fishing scenes and daily life, mainly from the early 20th century, before Beesands lost houses to wartime bombing.

Beesands and Hallsands from The Cricket Inn, Beesands.

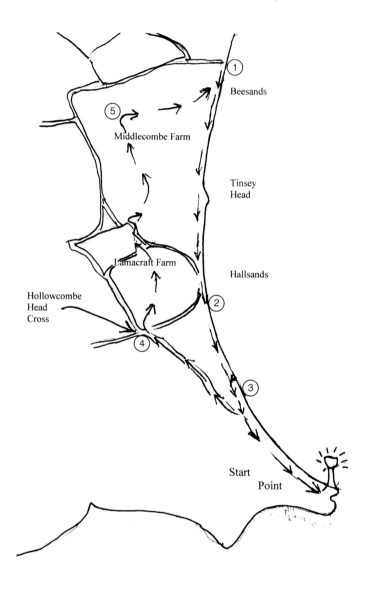

Beesands

Middlecombe Farm

Tinsey
Head

Lamacraft Farm

Hallsands

Hollowcombe
Head
Cross

Start

Point

2. DARTINGTON FROM THE COTT INN, 5km (3¼ miles).

Start/parking: roadside parking (with care please) in Dartington village near Cott Inn. SX787619.
Suitable for: all.
Terrain: footpaths and lane. No long or really steep slopes.
Stiles: 0.
Dartington Hall and Gardens: 01803 847012. www.dartingtonhall.org.uk (Walking groups, must book in advance). £2 donation per person for visiting gardens, £3 per person in groups of 10 plus. Guided tours by appointment.
Dogs: Not allowed in gardens. Please use lane alternative and keep under strict control on estate.
High Cross House: 01803 864114. Open 3 May to 28 October, Tuesday – Friday 14.00-16.30 (and 10.30-12.30 19 July-2 Sept.) Admission charge.

Although short, this is an exceptionally interesting walk, with a delightful riverbank section. En route, we visit Dartington Hall, one of England's finest late medieval buildings, set in a beautiful mature garden, noted for its sculptures. By complete contrast, High Cross House is one of the best examples of the 1930s International Modern style and is filled with excellent paintings, ceramics and furniture of that period.

Allow time too to visit the Cider Press Centre, which has a wide range of attractions, including a bazaar, restaurant, bookshop, pottery, wood turning, and galleries. Finally, the Cott is one of England's oldest inns and of exceptional interest.

1. Start: From the Cott Inn, follow the pavement downhill to Shinner's Bridge. Cross the Totnes road by the zebra crossing to the right of the roundabout to enter the Cider Press Centre, with its signposted collection of attractions.

2. 0.25km (300yds): Take the footpath signed for High Cross House and Dartington Hall. Start walking uphill and only 100m ahead, bear right at the sign for additional parking at a wooden gate. Follow the lane ahead past Foxholes to High Cross House.

High Cross House, including its fittings and many of its furnishings, was designed by Swiss-American architect William Lecaze in the bold, rather stark, geometric style of the Thirties. The art collection originally belonged to Leonard and Dorothy Elmhirst of New York, who bought Dartington Hall Estate in 1925 and here fulfilled their vision of rural regeneration and promotion of arts and crafts.

As well as early Chinese and Korean pottery, there are first class modern ceramics by Bernard and David Leach, Shoji Hamada and others. The paintings

5

include works by Ben Nicholson, Alfred Wallis, Winifred Nicholson, Christopher Wood, Elisabeth and Cecil Collins and Mark Tobey.

Follow the roadside path uphill and branch right as signed for 'Dartington Hall via Gardens'. (If you have a dog, continue on the roadside path and rejoin the route at point 3). It is a real privilege to visit these gardens, with their mature specimen trees and flowers, offering colour and interest through the year. Take time to explore and discover the several sculptures, which include works by Henry Moore and Peter Randall-Page. Dartington ask for a £2 donation (there are boxes at the entrance and the exit).

Walk on to the hall (circa 1399), which stands at the south end of what was the largest courtyard in England before the 16th century. The hall itself is on the grandest scale. The entrance arch, with Richard II's White Hart emblem, and the superb hammer beam roof, are particularly splendid.

3. 1.5km (1 mile) Leave by the arched entrance. Cross the road and walk ahead as signed for Park School. At the next junction, bear right for Park Road and Park

Dartington Hall and Gardens

School. Walk past the school to the turning circle at the end of the lane. Take the woodland path in front of you. Leave the wood by steps. Follow the field edge downhill, keeping the hedge on your left. Go through the gate. Walk ahead and turn right to join the riverbank path, a permissive route belonging to Dartington Hall Estate, which asks us 'respect, protect and enjoy' it. South Devon Steam Railway trains on the opposite bank make an impressive addition to the idyllic scene. Swans and ducks often grace the river. Look out too for rising trout.

4. 3.2km (2 miles) The path joins the lane from Dartington Hall. Continue ahead for 300m and turn right onto the cyclepath. Walk ahead to the point where the path meets the Totnes road by the old mill, with its overshot waterwheel. Cross the road with care and take the signed footpath uphill through the trees. The path emerges by houses. Bear left past them and then right onto the lane. 250m ahead is the Cott Inn.

Built in Edward II's reign (1284 - 1327), the Cott has been licensed since 1320, making it one of the oldest inns in England. According to the landlord, the heavily beamed bar features two inglenook fireplaces, whilst the thatched roof is said to be one of the longest in the country, covering both the original inn at the upper end of the building and what was the shippon (cow shed) and piggery until 1948 at the lower end. Running an inn the size the Cott now is must be a demanding job, but it is interesting to see that Thomas Searle managed to combine being landlord here with farming and fellmongering (dealing in skins and hides) in the 1850s.

The Cott is associated with Johannes Cott, who became a Freeman of nearby Totnes in 1333 and used to transport the produce of his mines and farms past the inn to the thriving inland port of Totnes. As an English name, Cott derives from the Old English *cot,* signifying a cottage. The Ordnance Survey map shows that the Cott Inn is located in Cott, Dartington. Devon has two further places called Cott, one at Uplowman near Tiverton, one at Georgeham near Barnstaple. The Georgeham Cott was probably the 14th century home of one John de Cotes, according to *The Place Names of Devon,* again underlining the association of a personal name with a place name.

Dartington from the Cott Inn.

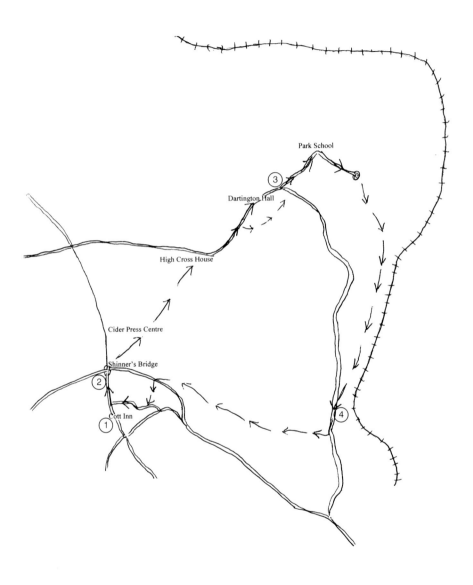

Park School

3

Dartington Hall

High Cross House

Cider Press Centre

Shinner's Bridge

2

Cott Inn

1

4

3. DITTISHAM TO THE ROYAL CASTLE HOTEL, DARTMOUTH, VIA THE DART VALLEY TRAIL, 5.6km (3½ miles) or 7.2km (4½ miles).

Start: Dittisham, Ferry Boat Inn.
Parking: car park in Dittisham, SX867548, 100m uphill from point 2.
Alternatively, park in Dartmouth and take the ferry to point 1.
Suitable for: anyone able to climb steep slopes.
Terrain: well signed paths and lanes. Two steep ascents and descents.
Stiles: 5
Ferries: Dartmouth/Kingswear continuous daily service. Greenway/
Dittisham daily (check on 01803 844010), Dittisham/Dartmouth 2 March
to end October (check on 01803 833206 0781001108).
Trail leaflets: from Dartmouth TIC, 01803 834224.

Following on from walk 9, Kingswear to Dittisham, this route gives a different perspective on the Dart Valley and the excuse for another river trip. Wonderful views compensate for two stiff climbs. Allow extra time for visiting. Dittisham is an especially attractive village and Dartmouth one of England's most ancient and interesting ports.

1. Landing at the Ferry Boat Inn (see walk 9), push uphill past pretty stone and slate cottages. Look out for plum trees, survivors of a long village tradition of growing fruit first brought by a German vessel. Turn left at the White House.

2. 250m Follow the Dart Valley signs uphill. Enjoy the marvellous view of Broad Reach, Greenway, the railway viaduct and on to Torbay. Reaching the lane, turn left. Ahead is the beacon on Fire Beacon Hill – built in 1988 to celebrate the 400th anniversary of the Spanish Armada's defeat. Chose either the bridleway to Old Mill Creek, or the footpath. The bridleway is the most direct route, though liable to be wet underfoot. The footpath, which is 1km (¾ mile) longer and includes several stiles and a steep descent, offers fine views of the creek. Both routes are enjoyable and well signed, but it is wise to check progress against the Ordnance map.

9

3. 1.25km (¾ mile) The bridleway begins by following the lane and passes Bozomzeal after 300m. This building began as a monastery and was later a medieval hall house – open to the roof, with its fireplace in the centre of the building. At the end of the lane, continue ahead as signed downhill through fields and gates and on through the wood, past the path junction, to Old Mill Creek. The longer footpath takes a SE course through fields. Turning west, it runs parallel to Old Mill Creek and continues through woods. It joins the bridleway 600m short of Old Mill Cottage.

4. 3.75km (2¼ miles) or 4.75km (3 miles) Cross the bridge at Old Mill Creek and note the limekiln opposite the old mill. Head up the steep lane as signed. Reaching the summit, turn right at the cul de sac sign. Cross Archway Road and then the main road. Walk on to St Clement's Church, the heart of Saxon Townstal. Typical of many Devon coastal settlements, Townstal was placed well inland to hide it from seaborne raiders. The *Domesday Book* of 1086 described Townstal's four smallholders, five villagers and two slaves. Dartmouth did not then exist, but rose to prominence in the early Middle Ages, when it was the assembly point for the Second and Third Crusades. It was incorporated in 1341.

5. 4.75km (3 miles) or 5.75km (3½ miles) Head downhill from the post office opposite the church. Take the lane with a No Entry sign. Follow the Trail signs down to the harbour. The Royal Castle Hotel faces the inner harbour.

It is much older than its handsome early 19th century façade suggests. Dartmouth grew prosperous on seaborne trade, especially the wool trade and the hotel began in 1639 as two houses, built by William Barnes and Joseph Cubitt, merchants – the Quay has one of England's best collections of 17th century timber framed merchants' houses.

However, some of the hotel's roof beams — recycled ships' spars — may predate the 17th century. During the 18th century, one of the merchants' houses was known as the New Inn. By 1777, both houses were combined, with a brew house and stables at the rear. The Customs and Excise held a sale at the Castle Inn that year of 'A quantity of Bordeaux Claret and French White Wine, Duty free and sufficient to raise £353 payment of salvage' – an interesting insight into the life of a maritime community.

The remarkable top-lit staircase hall with its magnificent bell board was built in the old courtyard between the two buildings in 1835, when a third floor, the Doric columns at the front entrance, the facade and the castellations appropriate to its name, were all added.

A new turnpike road arrived; the Castle prospered as a coaching inn, often mentioned in local newspapers such as *The Exeter Flying Post*. It is said to be

Dartmouth, as seen from Kingswear.

haunted by a phantom coach, which rumbles through the building after midnight. The coach is probably pre-1864, for the Dartmouth and Torbay Railway opened that year and the landlord of the Castle, Mr. Stone, sold 'two omnibuses by auction, an open dray, several pair horse and leading harness, horse clothing and twelve useful horses in seasoned condition, discontinued from running between the Brixham Road Station and Dartmouth in consequence of the opening of the railway line.'

The inn restyled itself as a hotel. Visits by the Prince of Wales and his eldest sons in the late 19th century boosted its status still further. It became the Royal Castle Hotel in 1902. Prince Charles and Prince Andrew have visited the hotel, which was a film set for Agatha Christie's *Ordeal by Innocence*. Other visitors include the seafarers Sir Francis Chichester, Chay Blyth and Alec Rose and film stars Cary Grant, Gregory Peck, Diana Dors and Faye Dunnaway. The Royal Castle has a wealth of historic artifacts, including swords and muskets. The 300-year-old range in the bar is still used for spit roasting.

Dartmouth has many other fascinating buildings, including the Butterwalk (1635). St Saviour's medieval church has a particularly splendid rood screen and decorated pulpit. Note too the fine brass of John Hawley. Four times the local MP and fourteen times Mayor, a licensed privateer and one of the chief commanders harrying the French, Hawley not only financed the church, but built the first fort which became the Dartmouth Castle we see today.

Dittisham to the Royal Castle Hotel, Dartmouth, via the Dart Valley Trail.

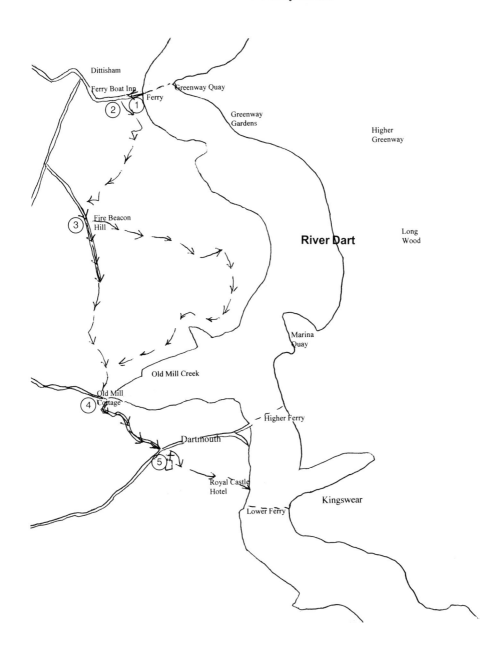

4. EAST PRAWLE AND START POINT FROM THE PIG'S NOSE, EAST PRAWLE, 14.5km (9 miles).

Start/parking: East Prawle SX782365.
Suitable for: anyone who can manage steep slopes
Terrain: well-beaten coast path, footpaths and quiet lanes. Two steep ascents, one sharp descent.
Stiles: 3.
Start Point Lighthouse: Normally open Easter to end September. Daily during July and August (11am-5pm) and Wednesdays, Thursdays, Sundays, Bank Holidays and school half-terms for the rest of the time. Confirm on 01803 770606. www.trinityhouse.co.uk

Our walk takes us by quiet inland paths and lanes to one of the most dramatic sections of the coast path. Choose a clear day to enjoy the superb views of Start Bay and Start Point.

Start's geology is fascinating. The series of low cliffs west of Start Point are really raised beaches at the fourteen foot and five foot levels, showing what the coastline was at different stages in geological time. That time extends back to the Devonian period in the schist cliffs behind.

Schists are unlike any other rocks found in Devon, they contain no fossils, and thus their age can only be assessed indirectly. Highly resistant rocks, they form spectacular headlands at Start Point and Bolt Tail. Standing as the southern rampart of Devon both geographically and geologically, they extend beneath the Channel, both westwards and southwards.

Geological maps show the 'Start Boundary Fault', cutting right across the southern tip of Devon, from Hallsands in the east to Hope Cove in the west. This line separates the schists from softer and younger Meadfoot slates to the north. The Meadfoot slates have eroded faster than the schists and the Dartmouth slates that form the next band of rocks to the north. This sandwich structure of rocks gives the South Hams its outline – broad to the north and at the tip, narrower in the middle. Nowhere can this outline be better seen than from Start Point.

1. Start From the parking area in East Prawle, face the Pig's Nose Inn. Turn right, and then follow the lane to the left. Turn first right and continue uphill. At the telephone box, turn right and follow the track ahead. The track becomes a path and follows the edge of a field to a metal gate. Turn right here at the sign for Lannacombe Green and Woodcombe Sand. Follow the track around a bend to a wooden gate. The path divides. Walk ahead for Lannacombe Green, then immediately left across a field. Turn right onto a concrete track and follow the

13

Lannacombe Beach

bridleway signs around the buildings (Higher Borough). Again, the path divides. Keep right on the signed public bridleway and follow the blue arrows along fields and tracks. The bridleway descends steeply to a tarred lane.

2. 3.5km (2¼ miles) Turn right and walk past the old mill house. Turn right at the next junction. 25m ahead the lane divides. Bear left and uphill to Hollowcombe Head Cross. Walk ahead for South Hallsands. Ignore the turn for Lamacraft Farm.

Trout's Holiday Apartments offer refreshments. See the ruins of South Hallsands from the viewing platform opposite. (Walk 1 gives a full description of how this village was washed away by the sea).

3. 5.5km (3½ miles) The path rises steadily towards the car park. Continue down the tarred drive (signed 'Lannacombe 2½') towards Start Point lighthouse, which appears less than its 87ft (28m) from the sheltering landward side.

Start Point Lighthouse

14

4. 7.25km (4½ miles) The next coast path sign tells us we are 462 miles from Minehead at the start of the South West Way. Either branch off immediately here or extend your walk to the lighthouse.

'Start' is derived from the Old English word *steort*, meaning a tail. A glance at the map shows how apt this is. Start Point has claimed several shipwrecks and many lives. The worst disasters occurred during the Great Blizzard of 1891, when fifty two people died.

The coast path crosses the ridge of rock leading to Start Point and opens onto a wonderful view of the lighthouse. Please take care on the next section – it is high and on a steep slope. Parts of the cliff are unstable, keep to the path, which climbs over rocks at Peartree Cove, but follows a gentle course to Lannacombe and on to Woodcombe Sand.

5. 12.25km (7½ miles) From Woodcombe Sand, either cut inland to East Prawle via Woodcombe or follow the coast path for another 1.5km (1 mile). The latter is tougher, but more interesting and the same distance. Beyond Malcombe House the path divides. Bear right and uphill for East Prawle. After 250m, turn right and up steps. Climb the very steep hill and turn right into the track. Keep right on to the Pig's Nose.

This delightful inn dates from the 16th - 17th centuries. It was recorded as the Union in 1857, but was re-named after the Second World War. The derivation is not the same as the Pig and Whistle at Littlehempston near Totnes, which is most probably from the 17th century phrase *To go to pigs and whistles*, meaning 'to go to ruin' – possibly as a result of overindulgence at inns. Rather, the Pig's Nose is named after a nearby coastal headland of the same name. Close to it are Ham Stone and Gammon Head.

Surprisingly, East Prawle was the scene of mayhem and bloodshed in 1872 when an Italian sailor, Salvatore Ilavi, ran berserk and was cut down by local Coastguards. Ilavi was aboard the brig Maria Theresa, homeward bound for Genoa. He and the rest of the crew rowed to safety after their vessel foundered on Brimpool Rocks. Eleven of the men sheltered at the Union Inn.

The trouble began that night when Ilavi grabbed a knife and started stabbing his shipmates. The landlord called some of the Coastguard and Ilavi ran away. Reaching the Coastguard station, he stabbed the duty Coastguard and his wife. When another Coastguard appeared, Ilavi stabbed him too.

Two more Coastguards eventually cornered him. John Sergue was armed with a cutlass, Henry Willcocks with a sword-stick. Ilavi flung himself at them and lashed out with his knife. One thrust hit Sergue, but deflected off his coat button. Sergue struck his assailant on the forehead and they wrenched the knife from Ilavi. A thrust from Willcocks's sword stick in the back killed the Italian, according to the post-mortem.

The inquest found that, while Sergue and Willcocks 'exceeded their duty, yet morally considered they had done their duty and the deceased died from a wound given by Willcocks accidentally while attempting to disarm the man.' All Ilavi's victims eventually recovered. Ask for a description of the incident whilst you enjoy a quiet pint.

East Prawle and Start Point from the Pig's Nose, East Prawle.

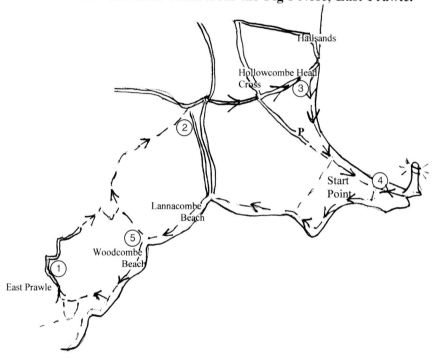

5. FROGMORE CREEK AND THE MILLBROOK INN, SOUTH POOL, 8km (5 miles).

Start/parking: roadside parking across creekhead bridge in Frogmore, SX775425. Please park carefully and do not block residents.
Suitable for: all.
Terrain: well marked footpaths. Short road sections – care needed. Largely level, with one steady climb.
Stiles: 11, including two high ones.

*Special notes: part of this route is along the foreshore of Frogmore Creek and should not be attempted two hours either side of high tide. It can be slippery at any time. Bring binoculars to study the birds.

Like the Breton coast across the Channel, Devon's south coast is deeply incised with beautiful estuaries and creeks that offer safe and sheltered havens for boats and wildfowl alike. Frogmore Creek, off the Kingsbridge Estuary, is one of these havens and is best seen from the footpath included in this walk. This

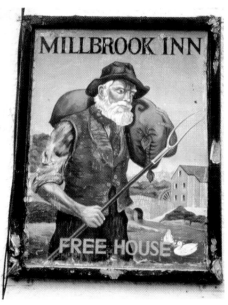

is a tranquil place indeed: commercial boat traffic has gone from both estuary and creek and the slate quarries are closed.   The walk back to Frogmore, via a lush green valley and a green lane, is equally peaceful.
1. Start/parking: Recross the creekhead bridge and enjoy the view. Double check that the tide is not right in – if it is, visit the Millbrook Inn first and start your walk later to avoid wet feet! Turn left onto the main road. 300m ahead turn left at the public footpath signed for Frogmore Creek and West Charleton. This crosses a field and then follows the creekside along a line of very low cliffs. Walk on along the edge of meadows and cornfields, where a wide grassy margin has been left to both promote wildlife and reduce erosion through run off from the fields. Butterflies, wildflowers and birds are thriving.
2. 2.5km (1½ miles): The footpath turns left to meet the foreshore. Turn

17

sharp right and follow the foreshore path as signed, taking great care over the rocks, especially if they are still wet. After 250m we are obliged to turn right and uphill as there is no right of way any further along the foreshore – as an unmistakable sign reminds us.

Take the path uphill through Geese Quarry Wood – the quarries were conveniently close to the creek for direct water transport. Emerging from the wood we meet a rough track. Follow the track ahead to the fire beacon, keeping the medieval tower of West Charleton church on your left. This beacon celebrated the Millennium. At the time of writing, it had been lit on New Year's Eve in 1999 and 2000 and on 3 June 2002 – the anniversary of English ships concentrating at Plymouth to drive off the Spanish Armada in 1588.

Leave the track and take the signed public footpath across the field. At the end of the field turn left as signed. Cross the stile in the hedge on your right and then bear left to meet a lane at an iron gate. Turn right and follow the lane up to the main road.

3. 4km (2½ miles): Turn left onto the road and almost immediately cross over into the signed footpath opposite. Follow the path between houses to a wooden gate. Walk ahead along the grassy track. Skirt the Grange as signed. Cross a stone stile and continue ahead at the next waymark through a meadow to a high stone stile.

4. 5.25km (3¼ miles): Turn right into the track, a green lane with characteristic high Devon hedgebanks, and rich with wildflowers. Before Devon lanes were tarred, they would have all looked much like this one, but often muddier and more rutted by horses and carts.

Where the hedgebanks break, there are magnificent views out onto the Kingsbridge Estuary. Ignore the first two turnings to the right, but when our green lane joins another, head right and downhill to meet the thatched cottages of Frogmore. Follow the main road back to the creekhead bridge.

On the far side of the bridge is the lane signed for South Pool, a 1½ mile drive. The village is exceptionally pretty, with a handsome church and the Millbrook Inn in the main street well worth a short diversion.

Inns named after mills are not unusual. Devon has two called the Mill, plus the Mill on the Exe. The Millbrook Inn stands half way between the church and Southpool Creek by a stream that once powered the village mill. This is shown in the excellent sign, which — as usual with signs by local artist Stanley Chew — is packed with historic detail. Alas, the millwheel, the miller and his pitchfork have gone and the mill is now cottages. Resident ducks in the stream are often joined by moorhens and sometimes by egrets or even a kingfisher. A leat (watercourse for the mill) ran above.

Built of local stone, with oak beams, the core of the Millbrook (once the Union) Inn is 17th century, with 18th and 19th century additions. Period photographs show Kingsbridge and South Pool. The village appears to have changed little. Also of interest are the horse brasses. The ship's wheel came from the Reindeer, a paddle steamer that once ran on the estuary. Her photograph is there too.

The Millbrook maintains a strong tradition of pub games, with teams for darts, cricket and euchre, a card game popular in Devon. Try your luck at the hand made quoits game too and enjoy the wood stoves in winter or the patio by the Millbrook in summer. There are real ales from the barrel and food lunchtimes and evenings.

Frogmore Creek

Frogmore Creek and the Millbrook Inn, South Pool.

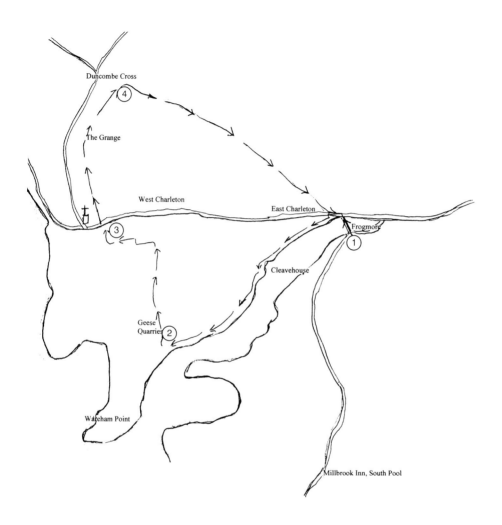

6. HARBERTON AND THE CHURCH HOUSE INN,
8km (5 miles).

Start/parking: Square by the church and Church House Inn, Harberton, SX777586.
Suitable for: all
Terrain: quiet lanes, footpaths and tracks. One steep ascent, one steep descent.
Stiles: 3.

Hidden among the folded green hills south of Totnes, Harberton has a remarkably beautiful church and one of the best church house inns in the South Hams. En route we have fine views of the pastures and woods of this fertile parish, and pass by two manors recorded in the 1086 *Domesday Book*. One, Great Englebourne, probably means 'bourne or stream of the English' and may have formed the boundary between the British and the invading Anglo-Saxons. Indeed, this is an ancient parish, older than Totnes, which was carved out of it in the 10th century and much older than neighbouring Harbertonford, which was only created from it in 1860.

1. Start/parking: St Andrew's is a splendid 14th/15th century church. Quite rightly, Simon Jenkins included it in his recent *England's Thousand Best Churches*. The first thing to notice is the 24m (78ft) tall tower of dark red sandstone, a fine landmark. By the porch is a Saxon Cross, decorated with palms.

Inside, the beautiful rood screen has pride of place. Although restored in 1870 with new panels, this is still essentially medieval – indeed, some of the original panels have been preserved behind glass and make an interesting contrast with the Victorian ones, which were painted on metal. Equally magnificent is the 15th century stone pulpit with carved figures, one of the best of its type in Devon. The font is of excellent Norman work, one of only twelve 'girdle' fonts in the county. Also of note are an Italianate Victorian memorial and the Royal Arms of Queen Anne.

Leaving the churchyard by the west gate, turn left and follow the alley footpath downhill. Turn left at the bottom of the path and follow the lane to a junction. Turn right and walk through the village, which has a number of attractive vernacular buildings, including Preston Farm.

The lane continues uphill, past handsome Tristford and then descends to Leigh Bridge. This crosses the River Harbourne that gave Harberton ('farm on the Harbourne) its name. The bridlepath short cut to East Leigh is overgrown and cannot be recommended, but the lane is a pleasing alternative.

2. 1.5km (1 mile): Turn left at East Leigh Cross for Harbertonford. Like neighbouring West Leigh and Hazard, East Leigh is now a farmhouse, but was classified as a 'manor' in the *Domesday Book,* William the Conqueror's great survey of his kingdom.

The lane bends left 350m beyond East Leigh. Take the signed public footpath ahead at the track entrance marked 'Foales Leigh'. When this track divides, keep left for Foales Leigh. Walk past the farm and continue ahead and downhill on a grassy track lined with hedgebanks and full of wildflowers in season. This leads to a wooden gate. Walk ahead as signed, keeping the field edges on your right. Cross Beenleigh Brook, where the old stone clapper bridge has been supplemented by a wooden one.

The footpath to Rolster Bridge is more apparent on the map than on the ground. Therefore, walk across the field ahead to a stile and cut diagonally right across the next field to a lane.

3. 3.75km (2½ miles) Turn left. At the next junction, turn left and downhill to Rolster Bridge. Rolster was recorded as a stone bridge in 1550, but its name is older than that, derived from the Old English *hrost,* meaning a beam. We may infer the original bridge was built of beams. Cross the bridge *Harberton* and turn left at the next junction, as signed for Eastleigh and Harberton. Walk on for 400m.

4. 5km (3¼ miles) The lane bends left by cottages. Walk ahead and uphill on the track, between typical Devon hedgebanks. Another track joins from the left. Do not take it, but walk straight on to Key's Englebourne Farm.

5. 6.25km (4 miles) It is possible to short cut back to Harberton from here via a rough track parallel to the river, but this is often waterlogged (even in summer) and cannot be recommended. Instead, follow the tarred lane to Bennett's Cross. Turn left for Harberton. At the next junction, turn left into the village. Take the second turning right and retrace your steps to the start for a well earned pint.

Harberton's medieval Church House Inn is built of stone and cob, a mixture of puddled straw and mud characteristic of Devon. Highly durable if properly made and kept dry with a good roof and sound footings, cob has excellent insulation properties.

Inside and out, the quality of the building is superb, especially the moulded oak beams. The magnificent oak screen was discovered after being hidden for centuries. In the main bar is a medieval lattice window, which contains glass said to be 13th century, a rare thing indeed, especially outside a church.

The abbot who ordered the building stipulated that it should serve as a Chantry House. Harberton had a relatively large religious community and the Great Chamber extends almost the full length of the inn, with what was originally the monks' chapel at the far end. There was also a small workshop for the monks in what is now the darts room.

Harberton and the Church House Inn.

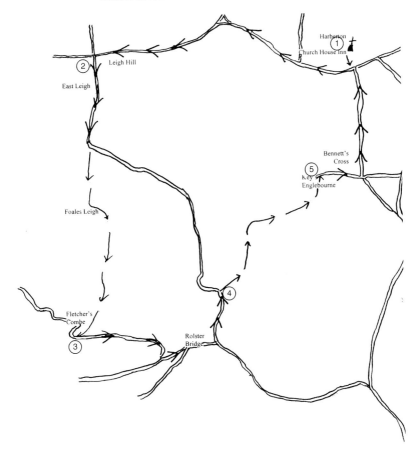

7. HOPE COVE AND THE HOPE AND ANCHOR 9.5km
(6 miles) or 7km (4½ miles) with short cut.

Start and parking: Outer Hope, SX676402. Alternative parking at Inner Hope.
Suitable for: anyone fairly fit.
Terrain: well defined coast path, inland footpaths and quiet country lanes.
Some ups and downs, but no long ascents or descents.
Stiles: 10.

This is a fine section of coast path, with much of interest, including the Iron Age promontory fort on Bolt Tail, the great arch of Thurlestone Rock and the thatched cottages at Inner Hope. The views to north and south are magnificent, especially from Bolt Tail. Choose a clear day to enjoy the walk at its best. This west-facing coast has seen many storms. Indeed, there are over a hundred shipwrecks in Bigbury Bay.

1. Start: From the car park by the Hope and Anchor, turn left onto the Coast Path. Follow this round to Inner Hope and divert up the street to see the cottages. Take the signed Coast Path up the steps by the old Lifeboat Station (1875). Continue on the well-beaten path out to Bolt Tail's promontory fort.

The projecting peninsula of Bolt Tail provided a classic position for fortification. The ramparts were built up on the landward side, probably in the later Iron Age, but the mounds within the fort appear to be natural outcrops of rock rather than barrows (burial mounds).

2. 1.25km (¾ mile): From Bolt Tail follow the Coast Path. Look back at the impressive rock formations, a blend of Start Mica Schists and Start Hornblende Schists. They dominate the coast as far east as Hallsands.

Ramilles Hole is named in honour of H.M.S. Ramilles, a ninety gun warship, wrecked here in a terrible storm in 1760. Walk on to Bolberry Down. A sign indicates a short cut to the Port Light Inn. Stick with the coast path to enjoy more of the views. The Port Light is on the edge of Bolberry Down car park. Take the lane 100m to the right of the inn. Follow it ahead and then downhill into Bolberry.

3. 4.75km (3 miles): Turn left at Bolberry junction. Turn right 50m ahead. Follow the lane downhill and then up. Where the lane curves right, take the footpath, signed 'Sweethearts Lane'. At the end of Sweethearts Lane, turn left on the signed path for Galmpton. 50m ahead, bear right for Galmpton on a clearly marked footpath. After crossing two stiles we come to a footpath junction. Either turn left here and make a short cut back to Inner Hope along the waymarked footpath or continue ahead to make the full circuit, which includes Galmpton Church and Thurlestone Rock.

4. 5.75km (3½ miles): To make the full circuit, continue down the broad track for 150m. Cross the stile on your left and cross the field ahead to the next stile. Continue ahead as signed over four more stiles to reach a small close of houses. Walk on to the lane junction ahead and turn left for Galmpton Church, designed in Early English style in 1867. The font and sections of alabaster reredos come from the old church at nearby South Huish.

5. 6.75km (4¼ miles): Exit the churchyard via an iron gate in the N.E. corner. Continue along the field edge to a track and a tarred lane. Follow the lane downhill to Pitchington Cross. Bear left, towards Thurlestone. At the next junction, turn left. Join the signed Coast Path for Hope Cove 25m ahead. This leads up a tarred track to a gate and the path proper.

6. 8.5km (5¼ miles): Follow the path southwards back to the start. Pause to admire the eroded arch of Thurlestone Rock. Thurlestone is derived from the Old English for 'holed rock'.

Thurlestone Rock has claimed its victims. A hurricane brought the Chanteloupe to grief here in 1772. A French privateer chased the George and Ann onto the Book

Hope Cove.

Rocks at Thurlestone in 1808. The privateer too was wrecked. These wrecks were joined by the German brigantine Theodor in 1874. As we walk down to Hope we pass Beacon Point, where the tug Empire Harry was wrecked in 1945. Her crew of nineteen was rescued by the Salcombe Lifeboat.

The San Pedro El Mayor (541 tons) was wrecked in Hope Cove itself in 1588 when she struck the Shippen Rock. She was the only Armada ship to be wrecked after completing the hazardous voyage around the British Isles. Many of the Spanish crew survived, but were shortly condemned to death. All were reprieved, but it was up to five years before they saw Spain again.

However, it is for Ramilles that this part of the coast is most notorious. Her loss at Bolt Tail in February 1760 was one of the greatest tragedies in the Royal Navy's history. Over seven hundred of her crew died. Twenty-six survived. Built in 1664, Ramilles was well past her prime. After repairs at Devonport, she

25

was ordered to join Admiral Boscawen's Channel Squadron. The stormy weather worsened and Ramilles leaked badly. All hands were ordered to the pumps. Tragically, her Sailing Master mistook Burgh Island for Looe Island. Hoping to make shelter in Plymouth Sound, he attempted to sail her round what he thought was Rame Head in Cornwall, but was really Bolt Tail.

The Hope and Anchor is 16th century in origin and has a fine collection of historic photographs of ships, shipwrecks and rescues. These include the beautiful Herzogin Cecile, queen of the grain racing clippers, wrecked at Starehole Bay in 1936. There are lifeboats new and old, a photo essay on the Coastguard and a portrait of a grey seal and her pup, born at Hope Cove.

The Hope and Anchor was recorded as such at least as early as 1857, but the story of the inn's name goes back much further. The earliest inns called the Anchor were monastic hostels. As with many early inn names the reference is Biblical: St Paul wrote of 'a sure and steadfast anchor of the soul, a hope.' (Hebrews 6:19).

Usually, inns called the Hope refer to this quotation, but at Hope Cove, there is also the place name to consider. The most probable derivation is from the Old English *Hop*. This signified a piece of remote enclosed land in the midst of fens or marshes, or a piece of wasteland. A third reason to call an inn Hope and Anchor is the sea itself. Landlords with maritime connections often named their inns Hope and Anchor to attract seafaring customers.

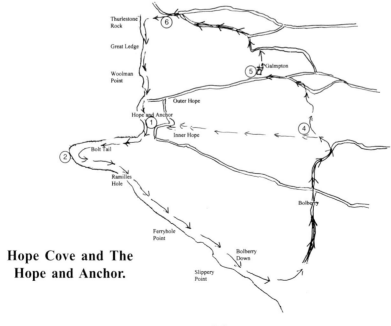

Hope Cove and The Hope and Anchor.

8. KINGSWEAR AND COLETON FISHACRE FROM THE ROYAL DART, 10km (6¼ miles).

Start/parking: Darthaven Marina car park, Kingswear, SX885512.
Suitable for: those who can manage steps and steep paths.
Terrain: well signed coast path, footpaths and quiet lanes. Several steep ascents and descents.
Stiles: 3.
Coleton Fishacre: (National Trust) Open daily except Mondays and Tuesdays 23 March -30 October, 10.30am-5.30pm; Saturdays and Sundays during rest March 10am-5pm. Phone 01803 752466.

Kingswear from the ferry. The Royal Dart is in the foreground.

Our walk follows the rocky, deeply indented coast between Kingswear, Froward Point and Pudcombe Cove. The gradients are tough, but the views are wonderful. Allow plenty of time for exploring, especially if visiting Coleton Fishacre. This handsome house reflects the best of the Arts and Crafts movement in design and furnishings. Built of local stone for the D'Oyly Carte family in 1925, it has much operatic memorabilia, especially of Gilbert and Sullivan productions. The gardens offer year round colour from a variety of rare and exotic plants.

Also of interest is a steam railway and station at Kingswear. The 80ft (24m) tall daymark at Brownstone has been guiding shipping for nearly 150 years. Nearby is a Second World War battery, now a rare and valuable historic monument.

27

1. Start: Turn right out of the car park and walk past Kingswear Station, restored to its old splendour. The Great Western Railway built the line here in 1864 as part of the 'Torbay Express' from London. Closed in 1972, it reopened the next year as the Dart Valley Railway. Steam locomotives and vintage diesels take period carriages to Paignton.

Follow the coastal footpath outside the Royal Dart as signed. Go through the arch and turn left up the steps. Ignore side turnings and stick with the coast path along a tarmac drive. Fine views of the Dart Estuary and Dartmouth Castle open up.

2. 1.6km (1 mile) Turn right at the coast path sign for Froward Point. This section (Warren Woods) is dedicated to Lt. Col. Herbert Jones, VC OBE, of Falklands War fame, who owned land here. We begin with a very steep descent to a small castellated building, once a mill. A steep ascent follows. The path is greatly enhanced by Monterey Pines.

3. 3.6km (2¼ miles) Brownstone Battery stands at Inner Froward Point.

Coleton Fishacre

Built in 1940 to protect the Dart Estuary, as well as Slapton and Blackpool Sands, it is one of the few surviving coastal defences from the Second World War. A display board maps the remains, including gun and searchlight positions. 300 soldiers manned Brownstone Battery to deter invasion. Later, the battery covered American D Day operations. Decommissioned in the late 1950s, it came under National Trust protection in 1981.

Several paths lead from Brownstone Battery. Follow the stony track towards Higher Brownstone car park for 150m only (unless you wish to shorten the walk

28

by going directly to point 5 via the daymark). Turn right at the coast path sign. The going remains tough, but the views are excellent.

600m short of the Coleton Fishacre turn is a path signed 'Car Parks'. Use this path to bypass Coleton Fishacre when it is closed and rejoin the directions from the lane by Higher Brownstone car park.

4. 5.5km (3½ miles) At Pudcombe Cove bear right into Coleton Fishacre. This is **not** a public right of way. Access is by National Trust membership or by paying at Reception. Details are posted on the gate. Rupert and Lady Dorothy D'Oyly Carte took Cornish valley gardens as their model for this delightful place, which shelters many rare plants and trees.

Follow the steep path up to the house. Coleton Fishacre was built of Dartmouth shale quarried in the valley and reflects the continuing influence of the Arts and Crafts Movement in its design. Inside, the flavour is Art Deco and there are many interesting features, including a wind dial and a three dimensional map of the very coast path we are exploring. A series of exhibitions are displayed in the house, including period photographs, embroidery and memorabilia from the D'Oyly Carte Opera Company. Art Deco furniture adds to the atmosphere, as does the music, played by a local pianist on Sunday afternoons.

Rupert and Lady Dorothy also enjoyed trips in their yacht and bathing in the pool at Pudcombe Cove. Domestic details were taken care of by a butler, a cook, a housekeeper and a housemaid. There were also six gardeners and a chauffer.

Continue to Reception and follow the tarred drive uphill. Turn left onto the lane for Higher Brownstone car park. For a good view of the daymark, divert into the car park. Built in 1864 as a navigational aid for Royal Mail ships sailing to the colonies, the daymark remains helpful in showing the entrance to the Dart Estuary.

5. 7km (4½ miles) Return to the lane, which becomes a public footpath. The path descends steeply from Higher Brownstone, and then climbs through pines to a tarred drive. Continue ahead (the footpath sign was damaged at the time of writing).

6. 8.25km (5 miles) Retrace your route from the flight of steps and the plaque to Lt. Col. Jones to the Royal Dart. It is essentially a handsome Victorian Italianate building, designed in the 1860s by Edward Appleton, under the direction of local magnate, Charles Seale-Hayne. Naturally, it specialized in accommodating railway passengers, some of whom were bound for holidays in the South Hams, whilst others were on onward voyages to many destinations.

However, the Royal Dart began as the Plume of Feathers in the 18th century. The landlord in the 1850s, Phillip Sandover, owned the ferry to Dartmouth. The name was changed to the Station Hotel after the arrival of the railway in 1864. It retains the Italianate station clock with 'GWR' (Great Western Railway). As the Dart Yacht Club met here, it was renamed the Yacht Hotel. When Queen Victoria patronized the Regatta, it became the Royal Dart Hotel. The Royal Family became closely associated with the area, especially Dartmouth and the Royal Naval College there. Royal patronage of local hotels also led the Castle in Dartmouth and the Seven Stars in Totnes to add Royal to their names.

During the Second World War, the Royal Dart was HMS Cicala after the Royal Navy requisitioned it as an HQ to control several Motor Gun Boat, Motor Torpedo Boat and Motor Launch Flotillas. In co-operation with the French Resistance, they smuggled secret agents into occupied France and smuggled Allied aviators back. Several French servicemen were stationed here, including Sub-Lieutenant de Gaulle (son of General Charles de Gaulle) and Lieutenant Francois Mitterrand – later President of France. There is a small collection of wartime memorabilia in the bar, including Morse code equipment, shell cases and Lt. de Gaulle's portrait. The river views, especially from the restaurant, are stunning.

Kingswear and Coleton Fishacre from The Royal Dart.

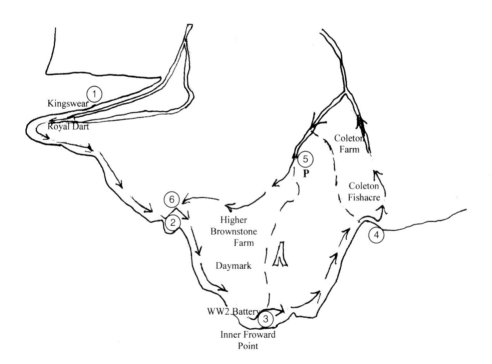

30

9. KINGSWEAR TO THE FERRY BOAT INN, DITTISHAM, VIA THE DART VALLEY TRAIL, 7.2km (4½ miles).

Start/parking: Kingswear Marina, SX885512.

Suitable for: anyone fairly fit.

Terrain: well marked footpaths and quiet lanes. 1 steep ascent.

Ferries: Dartmouth/Kingswear continuous daily service. Greenway/ Dittisham daily (check on 01803 844010), Dittisham/Dartmouth 2 March to end October (check on 01803 833206 or 07818001108).

Greenway Gardens (National Trust): 2 March Weds-Sat. to early Oct. 10.30am—5.00pm. 01803 842382.

Trail leaflets: from Dartmouth TIC, 01803 834224.

The best ways by far to explore the Dart Valley and appreciate its unsurpassed scenery are on foot and by boat. This delightful route combines both and can be joined to walk 3 from Dittisham to Dartmouth to make a 14.4km (9 mile) circuit that will take a full day.

Allow plenty of extra time for this walk, even if stopping at Dittisham, one of Devon's prettiest villages. There is much to see, including the smartly restored . steam railway station at Kingswear and Greenway Gardens. These woodland gardens, with their drifts of wildflowers and exotic plants, were once the home of Agatha Christie, and are now beautifully maintained by the National Trust. They

Ralegh's (Raleigh's) Boathouse at Greenway. In Agatha Christie's 'Dead Man's Folly', Marlene Tucker was strangled here.

offer further superb views of the river and much of interest besides, including sculptures, a tidal bathhouse and a restored Victorian greenhouse.

1. Start. Turn right into Fore Street. Cross the railway via the iron footbridge. The Great Western Railway built the line in 1864 as part of the 'Torbay Express' from London. The line was not continued to Dartmouth as first planned. This left Dartmouth Station oddly stranded and one of England's finest waterfronts uncluttered by a bridge, as we can well appreciate from this point. Closed in 1972, the railway reopened the next year as the Dart Valley Railway and features a variety of vintage locomotives and rolling stock.

Take the footpath on the far side between the river and the track. Continue ahead, as shown by the helpful blue markers that guide us through the entire route. Walk on to the higher ferry. Opened in 1831, it was then driven by a steam engine and carried horses and carriages. As today, the ferry ran on two chains linking Sandquay and Kingswear.

2. 1.25km (¾ mile): Turn right up the road as signed. At the toilets, turn right into Hoodown Wood. Turn left at the next path junction, 'Greenway Ferry and Maypool'. Cross the road ahead. Follow the Dart Valley Trail signs. Spring flowers, including primroses and red campion, bloom early in this sheltered microclimate and the furze (which hardly ever seems to stop flowering) is a blaze of yellow.

The National Trust cares for Long Wood, Noss Plantation and Cart Wood, which once supplied timber for shipbuilding and charcoal for Dartmouth smithies. Indeed, our track is called the Charcoal Cutter's Track.

Pause to enjoy the splendid views. Britannia Royal Naval College is the imposing red brick building across the river. Princes Charles and Andrew were among the line of royal cadets trained here. (Book a tour with Tourist Information). Below is a marina. It began as a shipyard, opened by Francis Simpson in 1891. During the Second World War, under Philip and Son, 500 men worked here – a German raid killed twenty in 1942.

The path climbs steeply out of Long Wood, 100 acres of semi-natural oak wood managed by the National Trust to conserve a variety of flora and fauna. Stick to the path as it levels off, and then descends towards Higher Greenway.

3. 4km (2½ miles) Follow the permissive path around the farm as signed. Cross another stile and continue to the lane. Turn left for Greenway Gardens and Ferry (as some of the old OS Explorer maps indicate). Just beyond Maypool – Francis Simpson's house and now a Youth Hostel – is a fine viewpoint and a plaque explaining the history of Philip's Yard and Greenway's connection with Sir Humphrey Gilbert. This Elizabethan sailor and explorer was Sir Walter Raleigh's half-brother and the founder of Newfoundland colony.

Divert right for 'Greenway Gardens' — the path is shown on the 2005 Explorer map, but not on earlier editions. On reaching the car park, turn left to explore the twenty eight acre gardens. Noted for their rare flowering trees and shrubs, Greenway's gardens were begun by Sir Walter Raleigh's other half-brother, John Gilbert. However, the house we now see at Greenway is Georgian and at the time of writing not open to the public. In a progressive gesture to green travel, the Trust offers reduced admission for anyone arriving by foot, bicycle or boat. Collect a map of the garden when you buy your ticket or show your membership card.

4. 5km (3 miles): If the gardens are closed (see Fact File), turn right to meet the lane. Walk downhill to Greenway Quay, with its 400 year old cottage. The ferry lands opposite the Ferry Boat Inn. The Inn stands next to the bell that summons the ferryman. A painting of 1884 in the bar shows the building as the Passage House Inn, an inn name that persists at Kingsteignton near Newton Abbot. Thomas Blampey was the landlord at Dittisham's Passage House in the 1850s, combining the roles of publican, ferryman and stonemason.

An early 20th century photograph proves the inn was called Turpin's for a time. Devon has two other inns called the Ferry Boat, plus two called the Ferry, one Ferryhouse and the more unusual Ferry Bridge in Dartmouth, celebrating the town's 'floating bridge', otherwise called the higher ferry, which we passed earlier at point 2.

Dittisham's Ferry Boat Inn is thought to be 17th century and features a large fireplace with blazing log fire and exposed ceiling beams. The wonderful views across the river are a special feature. Indeed, the inn is popular with visiting yachtsmen and walkers, as well as cadets from the Royal Britannia Naval College.

Being by the river, the inn is the centre of Dittisham's Regatta, held the middle Saturday of each August. Another maritime link is the brass bell in the bar from HMS Myngs, a destroyer launched in 1943. Her portrait hangs in the bar, along with naval insignia from many vessels.

View of the river from near Maypool.

Kingswear to the Ferry Boat Inn, Dittisham, via the Dart Valley Trail.

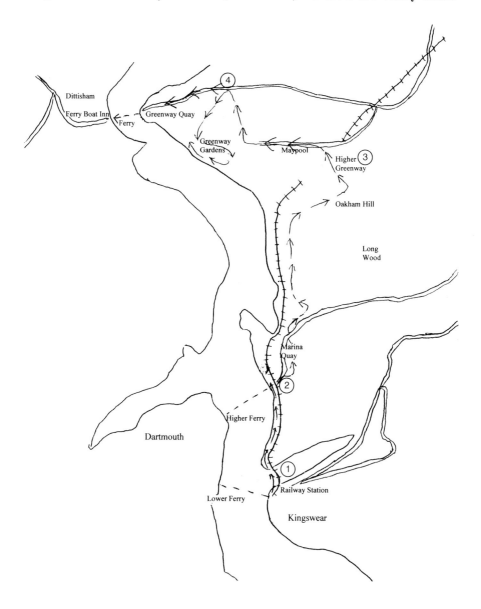

10. MODBURY AND THE EXETER INN. 4.75km (3 miles).

Start/parking: Poundwell Street car park, Modbury, SX657515.
Suitable for: all.
Terrain: footpaths and tracks. One steep ascent. One steep descent.
Stiles: 12.
Steps: 3.

We begin and end this pleasant and, by Devon standards, gentle walk in Modbury, one of the most handsome little towns in the South Hams. Its slate hung houses, mainly Georgian and Victorian, are characteristic of the area. A borough before 1238, its weekly market and two annual fairs were long focused on the wool trade. Modbury has a long history, as its Old English name suggests. This is derived from 'bury', meaning a fortified place and 'gemot', a meeting or assembly.

Modbury's two oldest buildings, The Exeter Inn and the parish church, are en route. St George's is a most interesting and attractive church and its broach spire

Modbury Parish Church

(an unusual feature in Devon) a landmark for miles around. Also medieval, the Exeter Inn was a Royalist meeting place in the Civil War, during which Parliamentarians defeated the King's men in two engagements at Modbury. In the second, the Roundheads chased their opponents down a track near the church still known as 'Runaway Lane' (part of our walk). They then went on to relieve the siege of Plymouth.

1. Start From the car park, follow Poundwell Street up to the junction of Modbury's main streets. Turn left up Church Street, past the White Hart (1827), the Exeter Inn and the former chapel of 1791. St George's is on the left at the top of the rise.

This large and exceptionally well lit church dates from the early 14th century, but was enlarged in the 15th and 16th centuries. It has a number of interesting features, including the old turret clock by the porch, made in Exeter in 1705. The best of the several memorials are the alabaster figure of Sir John Champernowne (1457-1503) in the south transept and Anne Downey and her family at the eastern end of the nave.

Leave the churchyard by the west gate and walk ahead, following the lane as it curves right. The cobbled path parallel to the lane was built in the 19th century to save the vicar from using what was then a muddy track.

2. 0.5km (¼ mile): Turn left into a signed public footpath at a stile. Keep the hedge on your right and cross two fields to enter Runaway Lane – which we have been walking beside. Royalists, besieged in a house near the church, made a hasty retreat down this lane, which very possibly was given its uncomplimentary name by their opponents. As they heavily outnumbered the King's men in this fight, it may have been more a strategic withdrawal.

Cross the footbridge and bear left over another stile. Bear right and keep the hedge on your right. Whilst Runaway Lane diverges uphill beyond the next gate, we continue ahead on the level path parallel to Aylestone Brook.

3. 2.75km (1¾ miles): Turn left onto the track in front of Cotlass Farm, which once had a corn mill. Follow the track past the farm, through a gate and uphill. Gaps in the hedge show fine views onto Dartmoor and the Erme estuary.

When the track meets a tarred lane, turn right. Only 25m ahead, bear left and up steps to a stile. Cross the field ahead on a signed public footpath, heading for the top left corner. A splendid view of Modbury opens out. Go through the metal gate as signed and keep the hedge on your right. Take the second metal gate on your right and cross the field ahead diagonally.

4. 4.25km (2¾ miles): The path goes through the first of two metal gates at Little Modbury. Follow the footpath signs carefully. Keep the hedge on your right through the first field. Cross the second field diagonally to a pair of new stiles. Now turn left, keeping the field edge on your left to a second pair of stiles. Cross over, turn right and walk to the field corner.

Cross the stile and follow the deep, shady sunken lane downhill. A typical 'holloway', this lane may be of considerable age. However, it is on a steep slope and based on soft rock. Thus, it would have eroded fast anyway, especially with the passage of people, horses and (when they arrived in Devon in the 18th century) carts.

Meeting a tarred lane, cross straight over and walk ahead for only 60m. Turn right up steps and follow the well-beaten path diagonally across the field to a stone stile. Walk ahead as signed past cottages to the car park and on to The Exeter Inn.

The Exeter is a coaching inn on the road to Exeter and this is the most probable derivation of its name. The core of the building, with its exposed beams, is 14th century, but the timber framed facade appears more recent. The Exeter was already licensed in 1563. At one time it was a court house, but resumed life as an inn in the 16th century. White ale, a concoction of malt, hops, eggs and flour peculiar to the South Hams, was brewed in the malt house behind the inn. Some of the old timbers were taken from here to build the present bar.

With the new era of turnpike roads and faster coaches in the late 18th century, the then landlord, W. Winsor, was keen to advertise the Exeter Inn 'late the Half Moon' in the *Exeter Flying Post* of 1796. He offered wine, liquor and accommodation, as well as 'neat post chaises, able horses and careful drivers'. No doubt, the horses were often led down the passage at the side of the inn now leading to the garden.

The painting above the fireplace bears the arms of the City of Exeter and its motto, *Semper Fidelis,* 'ever faithful' – the motto is repeated on the inn's new sign. Exeter's arms were confirmed in 1564 (the year Shakespeare was born) and the lion is that of Richard of Cornwall, who was granted the city and castle of Exeter by Henry III. Seventeen Devon inns have 'Exeter' in their names and the coat of arms is the most popular interpretation among sign painters. However, the Exeter at Topsham had a picture of HMS Exeter. Out of county, the Exeter Arms in Uppingham and Burrowden show Donald Finlay, later Marquis of Exeter, who won a gold medal in hurdling for Britain in the 1928 Olympics at Amsterdam.

Modbury and the Exeter Inn

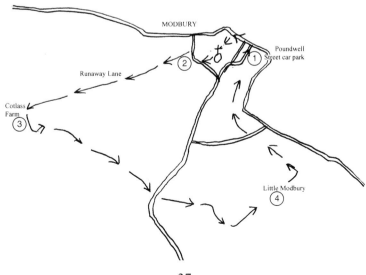

11. NOSS MAYO AND MEMBLAND, INCLUDING THE SWAN INN, 10km (6¼ miles).

Start/parking: Stoke Point National Trust car park SX556466.
Suitable for: anyone fairly fit.
Terrain: well signed coast and connecting paths and quiet lanes. Two steep ascents, two steep descents.
Stiles: 8 – no 'dog gates'

Our route takes us to the pretty village of Noss Mayo and Newton Creek, one of the most attractive of Devon's many sheltered anchorages. We follow the lane to Membland, the impressive remains of Lord Revelstoke's Victorian estate, and head down to the coast path. The going is tough at first, but much easier once we join the carriage drive Revelstoke built in the 1880s. Diverting downhill, we leave the drive to visit St Peter's, the ruined medieval church that once served Noss Mayo and thence cut back to the start. This is the complementary walk to number 11 in my original *Pint to Pint*, which also includes the welcoming Swan Inn, but explores Revelstoke's Drive to the west of Noss, around Mouthstone Point.

1. Start: Turn left out of the car park onto the lane. 650m ahead, turn right at Langdon Hill Cross for Noss Mayo. When the lane divides, fork left. Arriving in Noss, turn first left, then right along Creekside Road for the Swan Inn.

Like many heraldic names, the Swan has been known as an inn name and sign for centuries. It was first recorded in the 14th century and either referred directly to the royal bird or to a coat of arms featuring it, such as those of King Henry V (1413-22).

However, Noss Mayo's Swan probably dates from the beginning of the 19th century and its name is certainly apt for its waterfront location. During the Napoleonic Wars it was used as a holding prison for French captives who were incarcerated in the hulks in Plymouth Sound before Princetown Prison was begun in 1806.

Like many buildings in Noss, it belonged to the Membland Estate. The Baring family of banking fame, who bore the title Revelstoke, had suffered an earlier financial crisis and was obliged to sell the whole Membland Estate during the First World War. According to the 1915 sale catalogue, it was a free house with a bar parlour, taproom and bar. The rental was £20 per annum and it was sold for £625 to licensee Nicholas Bunker.

Photographs in the bar feature rowing races from the local Regatta. Two types of boat are shown: gigs and crabbers. Gigs are long rowing boats built for speed; their design dates from the days when West Country pilots raced each other to incoming ships to bid for business. Today, gig racing is a fast growing sport in local waters, but the sturdy, broad beamed crabbers (one of the most familiar working boats around the Devon and Cornish coasts) have their place in the Regatta too.

2. 2km (1¼ miles): Suitably refreshed, continue along Creekside Road under the handsome red sandstone tower of St Peter's, the Victorian replacement for the 14th century church we will vist later. Enjoy the view of Noss from Bridgend and take the lane signed for Membland.

Edward Baring's Victorian house became derelict and was demolished after the Second World War, but the attractive Membland outbuildings remain to indicate the style and comfort in which his family lived. These include stables (now apartments), whilst the Dutch gabled building opposite housed the electricity supply. Follow the lane ahead to Tea House Cross.

3. 5.5km (3½ miles): Cross the stile and take the footpath signed for Eastern Lodge. Perched on top of Beacon Hill opposite is the Tea (or Painting) House, that is often assumed to be one of Edward Baring's many creations, though it was recorded as *the Membland Pleasure House* in 1765.

Follow the field edge and cross the next stile on the left. Eastern Lodge is a Victorian hunting lodge of the Membland Estate. Would Victorians have approved the prominent nude statue in the garden?

Turn right and follow the lane for 300m, but pause to enjoy a fine view onto Lambside Farm and Dartmoor. Turn right onto the footpath signed as a link to the coast path and right again when you meet the coast path itself. There are great views east to Carswell and Keaton Coves. The path descends over a stile. Do not cross the second stile, which leads to Wadham Beach, but keep to the right of the fence on the coast path. The path climbs steeply up Beacon Hill, a wonderful vantage point.

Follow the coast path on what was Revelstoke Drive westwards to Revelstoke Park, which Baring might have recognized as a sound investment in caravans. Divert left and downhill as signed to visit St Peter's church.

Like St Werburgh's at Wembury (see walk 15), this church was built right on the coast and at a considerable distance — a mile and a half — from the community it served. Devon historian W.G. Hoskins suggested these sites were chosen because both churches were landmarks for shipping. The church guide speculates that they may have been defensive stockades dating from the time of Viking raids. However, if this were the case, why build churches that could easily be seen from a passing longship and thus invite attack?

The church is as Maurice Baring described it in the 1930s: 'nestled on the seashore, right down on the rocks, grey and covered with ivy, and surrounded by quaint tombstones that seem to have been scattered haphazardly in the thick grass and nettles.' Happily, it has been rendered safe and is now cared for by the Redundant Churches Fund. Open air services are held twice each summer.

4. 8.5km (5¼ miles): Follow the drive ahead from the church, past the caravans and into a pleasant woodland path. We emerge onto Stoke Down and then bear right and obliquely uphill at the waymark with a yellow arrow to rejoin the main coast path. 200m ahead, fork right at the waymark with a 'P' on one face. This leads directly to the start.

Noss Mayo and Membland including the Swan Inn.

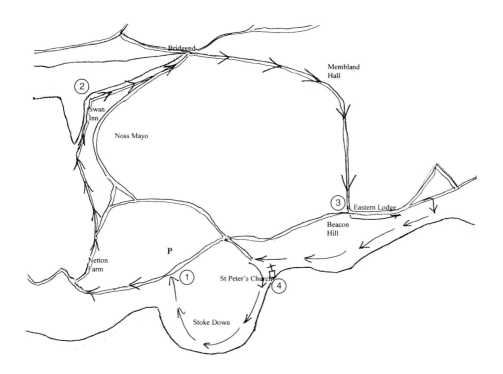

12. RATTERY AND THE CHURCH HOUSE INN, 5.7km (3½ miles).

Start/parking: car park by church and Church House Inn, Rattery, SX740616.
Suitable for: all.
Terrain: field and woodland paths, quiet lanes. Two steep ascents, one
steep descent.
Stiles: 1

   This is a good route to get away from summer crowds, or for a winter's day,
when daylight is at a premium and winds batter the coast path. There are great views
of South Devon's rolling hills and on to Dartmoor. You are not likely to meet other
walkers.
   The walk itself can be completed in less than two hours, but is better enjoyed at a
leisurely pace. Allow extra time to explore Rattery's Church House Inn, which is full
of interesting features. Devon's oldest inn, it is a world away from the hurly burly of
modern life. So are Rattery's late Norman church and the charming hamlet of Brooking,
which we visit half way around.
   1. Start/parking: Walk out of the church car park and turn left. 25m ahead, turn
left into a signed public footpath, which is a farm track leading to Allercombe. Look
back for a delightful view of the 13th century church tower grouped with mature
trees and the splendid vicarage.
   This is not quite how I imagined Rattery when I was a boy and the place name
first intrigued me. In fact, Rattery has nothing to do with rats. The name means 'the
place at the red tree'. It combines the Old English words *read* (red) and *treow* (tree).
Both words have given rise to surnames – Reed, Read or Reid (variously spelt) being
particularly common and derived from someone with red hair or a red complexion.
   At the cattle grid, continue along the track as signed. At Allercombe's first farm
building, the track divides. Do not enter the farmyard, but continue ahead on another
track, signed as a public footpath with a yellow arrow. As the track curves right,
follow the signed footpath ahead through a metal gate. Walk on through small fields
and enter the wood by a stile. A well established mix of oak, ash and hazel, with ferns
and wildflowers, this is a pleasant place indeed.
   Follow the footpath over the footbridge and through the wood to Brooking –
derived from the brook which runs through it. Cross the brook over a tiny hump
backed bridge by a ford.
   2. 2.5km (1 ½ miles) Walk ahead to the T junction. Turn left and walk on for
1.5km (1 mile) to Willing Cross. Enjoy a fine panorama of the South Hams as you
climb.
   3. 4km (2 ½ miles) Willing Cross derives its name from Margery atte Wille,

41

Brooking, one of the South Hams' small, hidden gems.

who lived in Rattery parish in 1330 at a spring or well (wielle). Atwell and Willing, like many English surnames, including Brooking and Ford, are rooted deep in the land. Take the lane signed for Rattery from Willing Cross. (It is best to stick to this quiet lane, the route via Willing Farm indicated on the Ordnance map cannot be recommended). The lane drops steeply beyond Parklands Farm, and then rises. Walk on to Rattery.

The Church House Inn was built either as a rest home for monks or a hostel for church builders, as the fine Stanley Chew sign shows. As ever, Chew packed a wealth of historical detail, based on his own researches, into the sign. The Church House is said to date from 1028, making it the oldest inn in Devon and one of the very oldest in England.

Other very ancient inns include the Turk's Head (Exeter), the Artichoke (Christow, Devon), the Falstaff (Canterbury), the Angel and Royal (Grantham, Lincs), the Star (Alfriston, Sussex), the Fighting Cocks (St Albans), the George and Vulture (London) and the Trip to Jerusalem (Nottingham). However, the title of 'England's oldest inn' is difficult to determine. For one thing, it is usually hard to judge just when a building was first used as an inn. Secondly, the earliest element in a building is often difficult to date – nearly all have been altered and extended over the centuries.

The Church House Inn (a Grade II Star listed building) has many interesting features, including one of the finest stone spiral staircases in England, a great open fireplace, a massive oak screen, oak beams and a list of Rattery's vicars stretching back to 1199, the year King John came to the throne.

The period photographs of Rattery, going back to 1887, add to the feeling of stepping back in time. This is aided by the absence of piped music and fruit machines – talk and the ticking long case clock a reminder of what all pubs used to sound like. The ghostly hooded figure of a man has been seen by several customers to walk the length of the inn before disappearing near the former priest hole.

The church is essentially Norman. Its font is one of the oldest in Devon. Like the nave, chancel and sanctuary, it probably dates from the 12th century. The tower, narrow aisles and probably the transepts were added in the 13th century and the chapels in the chancel in the 15th.

Extending right across the nave, the carved rood screen is 15th century and typically Devonian. It was ably restored by the Pinwell sisters in 1911. The church's handsome stained glass was installed in 1843, whilst the sgraffito on the walls is from 1870. Other points of interest include the sundial (1808) and the heavy oak door with its iron strap work.

Rattery and the Church House Inn.

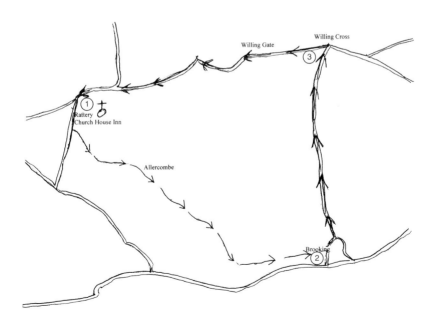

13. STOKE FLEMING TO STRETE FROM THE GREEN DRAGON.
7.5km (4¾ miles).

Start/parking: marked parking area in Stoke Fleming 50m uphill from Green Dragon, SX862484.
Suitable for: those who can manage steep paths.
Terrain: well signed coast path, footpaths and quiet lanes. Two steep ascents and descents.
Stiles: 7.

Following major work and re-routing, the new coast path between Stoke Fleming and Strete was opened in 2005. Thus, your map will not not show the path exactly as it now is if it was printed before 2005. This new path offers fine views of Blackpool Sands and Start Bay with its freshwater lake, Slapton Ley. Indeed, it really is coast path now and also greatly improved with top quality signs, gates and bridges. The connecting inland section of this circuit is by tracks and lanes, most attractive of all in spring when thick with wildflowers.

We begin at the Green Dragon, which has a good collection of period photographs, including ones of the building in the 1920s and in 1869. The Victorian photograph shows a modest pub. Henry Horswill, who was recorded as running it in 1857, was one of many publicans who supplemented his income with a second trade – shoemaking in his case.

'Licensed tippler' William Lidstone was the first recorded landlord of the pub

in 1607, though there has been a building here since 1170. Then, the lords of the manor owned it. Although opposite the church, the Green Dragon is unusual in never having been ecclesiastical property.

As for the name, the Green Dragon is derived from the coat of arms of the Earls of Pembroke and is not connected with the George and Dragon legend – though on George and Dragon inn signs, such as that at Dartmouth, the dragon is usually green. It is possible that the combination of green and dragon comes from stories of crocodiles brought back to medieval England by Crusaders.

Seeing the yacht adorning the weather vane outside the Green Dragon gives the clue to its sailing connection. The fascinating maritime photos, paintings, memorabilia and press cuttings in the bar describing the landlord's adventures soon confirms this. Peter Crowther has sailed the Atlantic single handed many times. On one voyage, the former yachting journalist brought his 1908 pilot cutter Golden Vanity safely to America in eighty eight days. On a more dramatic odyssey in 1996, Peter's Galway Blazer of Dart sank suddenly. He was lucky to escape with his life after a dramatic helicopter rescue – as his book recounts.

On a chill winter's day nothing is more welcome than the blazing fire in the huge hearth at the Green Dragon, whilst the patio is pleasant on a summer's evening.

1. Start: Walk uphill from the Green Dragon, past the parking area and take the first turning left (Mill Lane) as the road curves away right. Follow this pleasant green lane down to the tarred lane by Blackpool Farm and turn left. Arriving at the junction with the main road by a row of cottages, bear right onto the coast path. This runs parallel with the road and over a handsome stone foot bridge, one of the most noticeable improvements to the coast path hereabouts, relieving walkers of any need to use the road bridge.

2. 1.75km (1 mile) Turn right onto the lane ahead. The coast path now follows a flight of steps, but we push up the lane, past the cottages and on to Southwood Farm. Ignore the lane on the left and walk on to Narns Cross. Turn left and follow the lane into Strete, which retains an attractive medieval church tower, though the rest of the building is 1836. Walk on to the road junction. The King's Arms opposite has a handsome iron balcony and photographs of Strete from 1925.

3. 4.75km (3 miles) Watch out for traffic and turn left from the junction. 100m ahead cross the stile on your right and follow the coast path signs for Blackpool Sands. After following a course roughly parallel to the cliffs, the path turns sharply inland and drops very steeply into Landcombe, climbing equally steeply up the opposite side to a stile. (Please mind your footing). Cross the main road with care and follow the path right. Continue through fields as directed to a bungalow. Turn right and follow the track downhill to a stile and a stunning view of Blackpool Sands.

Now a popular family beach, Blackpool was a battle ground in 1404 when an invading Breton force which had landed at Slapton was defeated by local men. King Henry IV ordered a *Te Deum* sung in Westminster Abbey to celebrate.

4. 6.25km (4 miles) Cross the field ahead and follow the steps down to the lane, where we re-cross the stone footbridge. Instead of retracing your steps to Stoke Fleming, cross the main road and follow the new path between the road and the beach until it joins the pavement at a wooden gate. We only need keep to the pavement for 120m. Stop to enjoy the view of Start Bay. Re-cross the road and take the lane on the left at the yellow arrow. This leads directly to Stoke Fleming.

Overlooking Blackpool Sands.

Pause to explore the 700 year old church opposite the Green Dragon. Its most ancient feature is its Norman font, followed by the 13th century effigy of Lady Elynore Mohun. Next is the 14th century Corp brass, the second oldest in Devon. The Parliament clock dates from 1790, whilst the 1891 pulpit was carved by Miss Violet Pinwell when she was only seventeen. She also made the altar and altar rails, but the fine gull lectern was carved after her time in 1984.

Stoke Fleming to Strete from the Green Dragon.

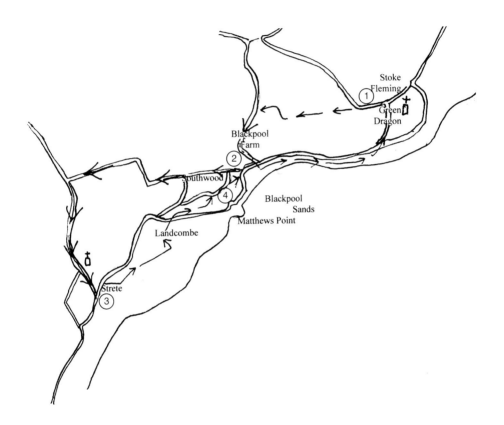

Stoke
Fleming
①
Green
Dragon

Blackpool
Farm
②
Southwood
④
Blackpool
Sands
Matthews Point
Landcombe
Strete
③

14. TORCROSS AND SLAPTON LEY WALK, INCLUDING THE START BAY INN, THE TRADESMAN'S ARMS AND THE TOWER INN, 13.75km (8½ miles).

Start/parking: Torcross, SX824421.
Suitable for: fit walkers.
Terrain: quiet footpaths, country lanes and coast path. Several ascents and descents, none arduous.
Stiles: 6.

This most interesting and beautiful circuit explores a remarkable section of the coast path, linked by field paths and rambling lanes. It includes four villages, two churches, a chantry and three pubs – though three more could be added.

We begin and end at Slapton Ley, the West Country's largest freshwater lake. Separated from the sea's fury only by a 4km/2 ½ mile long ridge of pebbles washed in from the Channel, the Ley is a fragile ecosystem. One of Devon's most important nature reserves, it is a haven for wildfowl.

Our entire route is within the area evacuated for D. Day training during 1943/44. Start Bay was chosen for its strategic position and similarity to the Norman coast. Victory came at a high price: the amphibious Sherman tank at Torcross car park is a memorial to the 946 men who died during Exercise Tiger in April 1944, when German E boats made a surprise attack on American landing

The Sherman tank raised from the seabed during 1984.

craft off the Devon coast. Retrieved from Start Bay in 1984 by local hotelier Ken Small, the Sherman is often decked with flags and flowers.

1. Start: From Torcross car park, take the signed path for Beesands. Turn right along the sea wall and on to a flight of steps. At the top, turn right. Ignore the first turning left. Take the second left 50m ahead and follow the coast path uphill as signed.

Enjoy the view of the coast and Slapton Ley. Formed about 1,000 years ago, the freshwater lake is under threat from rising sea levels, which may alter the local fauna and flora. Some species such as tufted duck, coot and moorhen that thrive now would probably leave if the sea breaks through. Freshwater fish such as pike would die. However, shelduck and other estuarine waders would thrive, as would salt tolerant plants.

Slapton Ley

The coast path skirts a vast, disused slate quarry before making a steep descent to Beesands. Walk ahead past Widdicombe Ley, a smaller version of Slapton Ley. At the far end of the village green turn right and walk up the lane. Follow the lane as it curves right and uphill. Do not take the first footpath on your right, press uphill to Beeson. Ignore the first lane on your right.

2. 3km (1¾ miles). At Beeson Cross turn right, signed 'Widewell 1m'. After 50m, fork left as signed. Fork left again at the yellow waymark. At Lower Widdicombe Farm, continue uphill as signed. At the next footpath junction, walk on for 'Widewell.'

3. 4.5km (2 ¾ miles) When you reach the lane, walk straight ahead. Follow on to Stokenham. The medieval Church House Inn, with its ancient beams, stands opposite the handsome church. Built of local slate, St Michael's is noted for its tall tower; superb 16th century carved and painted screen and Norman font.

4. 5.3km (3¼ miles) Walk up the lane to the Tradesman's Arms. The thatched half dates to the late 13th early 14th century; the adjoining Georgian half has a slate roof. Next door was Well Cottage, formerly the brewhouse, with its own water supply.

No doubt the inn was used by thirsty tradesmen who passed by on the busy route between Kingsbridge and Dartmouth. Thus, the Tradesman's Arms came by its name in a similar way to the Cott Inn, Dartington (walk 2), named after Johannes Cott, who traded at Totnes.

The excellent Stokenham sign shows a tradesman with his packhorse, bearing its load in panniers, supported on a wooden frame. This is historically correct. Before the era of turnpiked roads (early 19th century), most goods in Devon were carried this way. More recent history can be gleaned from the inn's collection of period photographs.

Retrace your steps towards the church and take the first turning left. Follow the narrow lane uphill to a junction. Continue uphill. Walk on to Frittiscombe.

5. 6.5km (4 miles) Turn right, signed 'Scrubbs Lane to Deer Bridge Lane'. Walk past farm buildings to a lane. Turn right and walk steeply downhill. 40m beyond Deer Bridge, bear right, signed 'Marsh Lane'. Follow on to a footpath junction. Bear left for 'Slapton Village ¼ m'. On reaching the lane junction, turn right into the village. Bear left up to Slapton Church, with its carved rood screen and 1766 Royal Coat of Arms.

The impressive 80ft high tower of Slapton's Chantry stands north of the church. Next to it is the Tower Inn, itself an ancient building with many interesting features, including beams and pillars, flagstones, settles and open fireplaces. The Chantry was built in 1372 by Sir Guy de Brien, lord of the manor and one of England's leading men during Edward III's reign. St Mary's was the last of several collegiate churches in Devon. They were minster-churches, with a number of priests forming a college and acting as missionaries in the surrounding area. All English chantries were suppressed by Henry VIII in 1545. A few fragments of the Chantry are incorporated in a house called the Chantry, which is probably medieval and part of the college buildings, but looks late Georgian.

6. 9.25km (5¾ miles) Follow the lane along the north side of the churchyard and under an iron bridge. Walk past the Queen's Arms (more temptation!) and turn left at Sands Road Corner towards Torcross. Walk past Slapton Ley Field Centre and turn right 80m ahead at the public footpath sign. Follow the footpath behind the farm as signed and walk on to the lakeside path. Turn left for 'Slapton Sands'.

7. 11.25km (7miles) Turn right at the lane and right again. Either use the official coast path alongside Slapton Ley or trail along the edge of the beach. Walk straight on to the Start Bay Inn, formerly the Fisherman's Rest and the Fisherman's Arms.

This thatched inn is said to be 14th century in origin. Appropriately for Start Bay, the new sign shows boats drawn up on the beach.

Period photographs in the bar prove that the exterior of the inn has not been greatly changed. As for the name 'Start', it is derived from the Old English word *steort*, meaning a tail or promontory.

Torcross and Slapton Ley Walk.

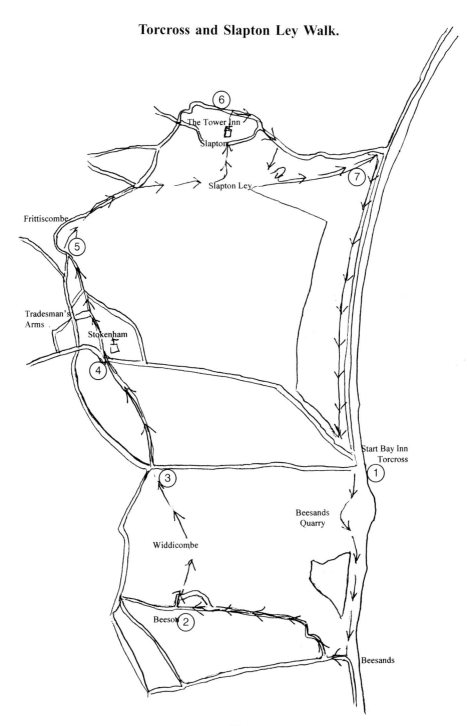

15. WEMBURY AND THE ODD WHEEL, 7km (4½ miles).

Start/parking: National Trust car park, Wembury Beach. SX518486
Suitable for: all.
Terrain: well signed footpaths, gentle coast path. One steep ascent, one steep descent in optional diversion to the riverbank.
Stiles: 7.

This gentle route starts near the Marine Centre at Wembury Beach, passes by the former millhouse (now a café) and follows the pretty Churchwood Valley to The Odd Wheel, well situated half way round. From there, the footpath skirts handsome Wembury House (1803) to one of Devon's most beautiful estuary views at Warren Point. The pleasant, largely level coast path back leads to Wembury Church. Noted for its monuments, St Werburgh's is dedicated to a Saxon princess. Its striking tower has been a landmark to mariners heading for Plymouth Sound and the Yealm estuary for seven centuries.

1. Start/parking: When driving through Wembury, follow the signs to the National Trust car park. Walk back to the entrance to visit the Marine Centre (free entry). Tableaux and a fish tank illustrate the riches of local marine life. Indeed, Wembury is a Voluntary Marine Conservation Area, with much input from Devon Wildlife Trust. From the beach shop and café opposite take the footpath alongside the brook. Reaching the lane, turn right. Walk past the telephone box and take the signed public footpath (part of the Erme/Plym Trail) for Ford. This path soon after divides in two – the upper path is for walkers and the lower (muddier) path for horses.

Reaching a lane, turn left on the Erme/Plym Trail. 100m ahead, turn right as signed. Just beyond Ford Farm the path divides. Keep right and uphill. Stay with the Erme/Plym Trail, using the stiles and waymarks to guide you across four fields to meet a lane, marked 'Train Road' on the Ordnance Survey Explorer map. Turn right and walk ahead to The Odd Wheel.

The Odd Wheel began as the Jubilee Inn. The name probably derives from George III's Golden Jubilee in 1810. Certainly, it was recorded as an inn in 1841, but Watneys changed the name after they bought the house, perhaps because they already had an inn called the Jubilee. It is said that The Odd Wheel got its unique name from the iron wheel with strange curved spokes, now found on the outside wall above the entrance porch and that this wheel was formerly used at Wembury Mill. Several other odd wheels, including cartwheels, decorate the bars. Local artist Edward Boyle painted the pleasing exterior signs.

Other English inns with 'odd' in their names include several Oddfellows Arms

(from the benevolent society of that name), an Odd Bottle, Odd House, Odd Spot and Odd Whim. There are several inns called the Wheel, including one in Truro, formerly a wheelwright's shop.

2. 2.2km (1½ miles) With your back to The Odd Wheel walk ahead, past the school and the Olive Tree Church. Take the footpath opposite the shop, signed for Brownhill Lane. When the path divides, keep left at the yellow arrow and climb the steps into the field path ahead as signed. Cross the field and continue ahead with the stone wall of Wembury House's grounds on your left. Cross a stone stile into a lane. Do not take the footpath to Brownhill Lane. Walk straight ahead. When the tarmac ends, continue on a track, as signed for the coast path. To your left are fine views onto Dartmoor and Noss Mayo.

3. 4.2km (2¾ miles) At the cottage the path divides. If you wish to get a good view of the many boats moored on the River Yealm walk ahead down the steep hill to the riverbank. Retrace your steps uphill to the cottage and bear left onto the coast path. This gives an easy, pleasantly level walk back to the start.

A small diversion to the church is well worthwhile. This was the little grey church by the sea where John Galsworthy's character, Soames Forsyte, makes a pilgrimage to the home of his ancestors in *Swan Song*. Its dedication is one of fourteen to St Werburgh, the daughter of Wulfhere, the first Christian king of Mercia.

There is much of interest inside, including the Royal Arms of George III and some good modern wood carving, but the monuments are especially splendid. Sir John Hele lies in the chancel, with the effigies of his wife and ten children. Lady Narborough 'Mightily afflicted with a cough and Bigge with child' is remembered in another monument of 1678 by the porch.

Follow the link path down to the car park.

Boats on the River Yealm — the view is well worth the short diversion from point 3.

Wembury and The Odd Wheel.

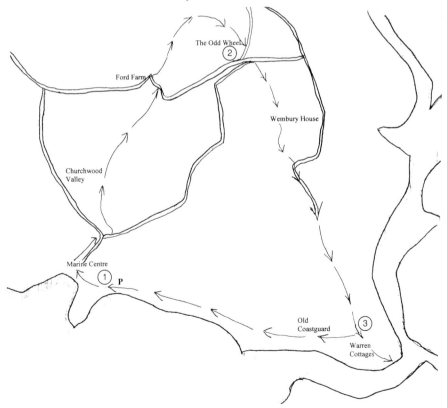

16. YEALMPTON FROM THE VOLUNTEER INN.
6.3km (4 miles).

Start/parking: roadside parking in Yealmpton (with care please). SX577517.
Suitable for: all.
Terrain: well signed footpaths and quiet lanes. One short, steep ascent.
Stiles: 3.

This gentle route begins and ends in Yealmpton by way of winding lanes, riverbank and field paths. The village has retained its own identity and the charm of its setting by the Yealm. The river name is Celtic, but Yealmpton ('farm on the Yealm') is a Saxon name as is Dunstone ('Dunstan's farm'), with its statue of St Dunstan, which we pass en route.

Yealmpton has what John Betjeman described as 'the most amazing Victorian church in Devon', with medieval brasses and an ancient Celtic stone in the churchyard. A short diversion adds 'Old Mother Hubbard's Restaurant'. This ancient cob and thatch building is said to be the home of the nursery rhyme's chief character. Her dog, with its bone, is on the roof ridge.

1. Start: Take the footpath opposite the Volunteer past the toilets. This leads down to St Bartholomew's. The church was rebuilt by architect William Butterfield in 1852. Kitley marble is used to good effect and the handsome design is characteristic of the Gothic Revival.

Look out for the Crocker Brass in the North Transept, showing a knight in armour. The Latin inscription means: 'Here lies John Crokker, Knight, once cupbearer and standard bearer of the most illustrious King Edward IV, who died 14 March A.D. 1508.' Even older is the Palimpsest Brass nearby, which dates from the time of Agincourt, 1415.

The Goreus Stone in the churchyard is of Cornish granite. It is thought to commemorate an ancient British chieftain, who embraced Christianity 1500 years ago. This suggests that there was a settlement here before Yealmpton gained its Saxon name.

The Goreus Stone

Leave the churchyard by the south gate and turn right into a signed public footpath, which leads through a park. At the far side of the park, turn left at the public footpath sign and follow the track through the wood to the old limekilns. Burnt limestone was widely used as a dressing in Devon to neutralize acid soils.

Do not cross the footbridge, but continue ahead, keeping the riverbank on your left, past Kitley Caves and under the dismantled railway bridge. Follow the pleasant bankside path to Puslinch Bridge.

2. 1.25km (¾ mile) Turn left, cross the bridge and turn left again up an unsigned lane marked *Unsuitable for Heavy Goods Vehicles.* Stay with the lane as it winds uphill. If you wish to make a short cut back to Yealmpton, take footpath 17 – otherwise, continue to Two Crosses. The bridleway that runs parallel to the last section of this lane was too overgrown at the time of writing to use, but the lane itself was so delightfully quiet with its flower rich hedgebanks that this was no loss.

3. 2.5km (1½ miles) Cross the B3186 with care and continue on the narrow lane opposite signed for Dunstone and Holbeton. Fine views onto Dartmoor open up on the way to Dunstone, an attractive hamlet with some interesting vernacular buildings, several of them thatched.

4. 3.4km (2¼ miles) Turn left at the junction in Dunstone. St Dunstan's statue is 100m ahead, high in a wall on your left. This was erected after the Second World War with the epitaph '910-988, A Great Englishman'. The patron saint of goldsmiths, Dunstan was made Archbishop of Canterbury in 961.

300m further on, turn left into an enclosed footpath, signed as part of the Erme Plym Trail. Arriving at a path junction, continue ahead. On your right, the Yealm roars over a weir. Follow the path along the edge of the depot. Cross a stile and walk ahead across a field to a stile and small footbridge. Walk ahead into an enclosed path. Leave this via a stone stile. Keep the field edge on your left and then cut diagonally right across two fields as signed on a well-beaten path. Cross another stile and continue ahead to a cul-de-sac. Cross over and walk ahead to the river. Follow the bankside path back to Yealmpton. Turn right at the road bridge and walk uphill to the junction.

To add a visit to Mother Hubbard's Restaurant, turn right and walk on for 150m. The original nursery rhyme was written by Sarah Catherine Martin in 1804. Old Mother Hubbard is said to be based on the housekeeper of the nearby Kitley Estate, where Miss Martin was a regular visitor. Her own life had a fairy tale flavour. She was proposed to by Prince William Henry (later King William IV), but they could not marry because of their widely different social stations.

Retrace your steps to The Volunteer, which has a collection of period photographs, some showing the village of a century ago, and paintings by local artists. Many inns around the country are named in honour of the armed forces, famous regiments, battleships, warplanes and local militia. The Volunteer is a popular name and refers particularly to volunteer regiments raised at the time of the Napoleonic Wars. Inns were often used a troop billets and recruiting centres. Sometimes they used the force of the press gang to find extra men, at other times mere persuasion, aided by alcohol and 'the King's shilling'. This was the subject of a comedy, *The Recruiting Officer,* by George Farquhar, first produced on stage in 1706.

It appears that the inn began as two cottages, one of which was a malt house. These two cottages later came under a single tenancy. At the height of the French invasion threat in 1806, the inn was known as the Rifle Volunteer, a name still found in several places around England.

Local inn sign artist Edward Boyle painted a soldier of the Napoleonic period on the excellent Yealmpton sign. However, there may also be an association with the South Hams Yeomanry, a regiment first raised some six years after Waterloo in 1821 and disbanded in 1838. During most of this period, troops were paid, but from 1827-31 they served voluntarily. In *Pigot's Directory* of 1830-31 the inn is recorded as the Volunteer and the name  has remained simply the Volunteer since then.

Devon has five other Volunteers. The Sidmouth Volunteer depicts a private of the 11th Foot, which later became the Devonshire Regiment and then the Devon and Dorset. At Exmouth, the sign shows a Lifeboatman.

With thanks to Bob Frederick and Chris Burtt for information about the Volunteer Inn.

Yealmpton from the Volunteer Inn.

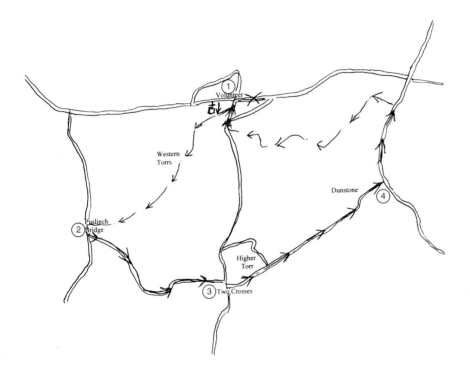